The voyage of discovery lies not in finding
new landscapes, but in having new eyes.

— Marcel Proust

That Perception Thing!

Dawn Brown

Creative Bound Inc.
Resources for personal growth and enhanced performance
www.creativebound.com
(613) 831-3641

ISBN 0-921165-76-5   Printed and bound in Canada

Many of the stories in this book involve real people the author has met in her life and career. To protect the privacy of those people, their names have, in most cases, been omitted and personal details have been altered in ways inconsequential to the story.

This book is not a substitute for professional psychological help. It is simply one step in the process of seeking a healthier way of living.

Production by   Baird O'Keefe Publishing Inc., *Publication Specialists*
                  Gail Baird, Managing Editor
                  Wendy O'Keefe, Creative Director

National Library of Canada Cataloguing in Publication Data

Brown, Dawn (Dawn H.P.)
   That perception thing!

Includes bibliographical references.
ISBN 0-921165-76-5

   1. Self-actualization (Psychology)   I. Title.

BF637.S4B76 2002   158.1   C2001-904179-9

In loving memory of my husband Laurence Cosmo, whose love and wisdom gave me the foundation to grow.

Acknowledgments

My gratitude goes to the following people. They have all contributed in some way to making this book possible:

- My children Layla and Jason have been my partners in learning, challenging and encouraging me to keep going. I have been blessed.
- My sibs Gail, Kaye, and Geoffrey, and my mother Viola have always provided much-appreciated love.
- Wanda Bowring challenged me to continue writing. Her magazine, *Energy Medicine,* was the vehicle that kept my writing going.
- Ann Fothergill-Brown's excellent ability as an editor is reflected in this book. She also provided me with the objectivity needed to complete it.
- Friendship from Musia, Isobel, Gail Carroll, Denyse and Ann T-B, and both Michelles provided support when it was needed.
- My OH Card friends, Ely, Joan, Sylvia, and Mo, provided me with a new way of looking at life.

- Over the years, my clients, people attending my workshops and lectures, and people that I've met in my travels have inspired me by allowing me the privilege of looking at life through their eyes. In turn, their appreciation has encouraged me to continue my work.
- CAPS (Canadian Association of Professional Speakers) has been a very supportive organization.
- Andre kept me on track and focused.
- Wendy O'Keefe captured the essence of perception on the book cover, and Gail Baird guided the book through the publishing process.
- Marianne Williamson introduced me to *A Course in Miracles* in such a gentle way.
- Kenneth Wapnick used his incredible gift as a teacher to help me see things differently.

Many writers and speakers have inspired me over the years. Their words have contributed to my voyage of self-discovery. If I've not acknowledged them, it was not intentional. They have my thanks.

Contents

Introduction

Arrows to flowers: That perception thing!

Many years ago, in a certain class, I had a group assignment with four classmates. As the professor was explaining the assignment, I happened to see Robin drawing arrows all over her paper. Intrigued, I demanded to know why she was drawing arrows. She smiled at my strong reaction and was about to answer, when Ron, sitting across from me, looked at me in shock and pointed out that Robin was drawing flowers. Upon realizing that we both were serious about what we had seen, we argued the point back and forth. Finally, Ron took the paper and turned it around. I suddenly realized that from where Ron was sitting, he *had* seen flowers. On the other hand, from my vantage point, I had seen arrows.

Since then, arrows and flowers have been powerful reminders for me of how a shift in perception can change our reality. Not only that, but "reality" for one person is not the same as "reality" for another.

Robin had indeed been drawing arrows. For her, they signified a need for direction in life. On the other hand, I had seen them as painful objects.

That point is important when considering the OH Cards. (But I'm getting ahead of myself. I'll explain the OH Cards in a moment.)

Back to perception and to my fascination with its creative forces.

Years after the gift of that initial insight, I had amassed a wealth of stories and metaphors to illustrate the powers of perception. I wove those into the workshops and lectures that I gave and the articles that I wrote. Then, the idea of pulling everything together into a book was born. More time passed, and with the book nearing completion, I still had not come up with a satisfactory title.

Around that time, I visited a friend I had met in Rhode Island. Although our backgrounds were very different, we had hit it off from the moment of meeting a year earlier. My friend took my quest for a title very seriously. She suggested that we take a walk and brainstorm ideas.

We met at her home, which turned out be a castle. As we walked around the neighborhood, she was able to tell me about the architecture of the other homes—the style, year of construction, history, cost, and, in some cases, the furnishings!

Then my friend eagerly showed me her dream home, describing it with great passion. She told me that the house had recently sold for almost $60 million. She said that she would have loved to own the house, and she lamented the fact that she had not been born rich. Clearly, since her family was "worth" less than $5 million, she could not afford the house.

I shrugged and said, "Ah, that perception thing. Some people would consider you rich." Joan became instantly excited. The house was forgotten. "That's it!" she said. "You've got the title for your book."

And so I did.

The book

In this book, I want to share with you the gift of seeing things differently.

I invite you to treat the book as a journey. On the journey, you will allow yourself the freedom to explore different ways of looking at the themes you encounter—themes that run through life. Every encounter is an invitation to meet yourself, free of the judgment that is so much a part of daily life. The main themes throughout the book will guide you in that process. Those themes are *love, forgiveness, gratitude,* and *being in the present*.

I've been gathering the stories and metaphors that illustrate the themes in this book over my entire lifetime. I've been writing the book itself for the past few years. Like a refrain in a song, certain themes repeat. They mark lessons that were repeated for me. I once read that lessons are repeated until they are learned. Well, I needed to hear those learnings again, to look at them in new ways.

You may find that this book works in the same way for you. The stories may touch you one way on a first reading. But if you pick up the book and reread a passage months from now, you may find new and different inspiration. I hope that my words, coupled with your personal exploration, will reveal your next steps and inspire you to take them.

The OH Cards

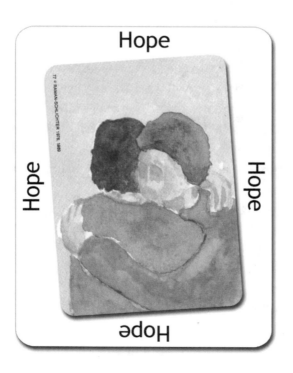

To help in your exploration, the end of each chapter features a pair of OH Cards (pronounced "oh" cards). OH Cards come in two decks: one deck with words, and one with pictures. Each deck contains 88 cards. The picture cards are slightly smaller than the word cards. When you put two cards—one from each deck—together, you combine word and picture to form a single image.

For years, I have used OH Cards to help myself and others draw from within what we may intuitively feel but have not managed to put into words. Although neutral in themselves, the cards assist in the projection of feelings and meanings. There are no good or bad cards, no right or wrong interpretations. The meanings change with the viewer and with the viewer's current feelings. Like the arrows/flowers that I spoke about earlier, viewers may have different perceptions of the cards.

I've selected 25 card combinations for this book. If you like, you can use them as a stimulus to examine further whatever thoughts and feelings have surfaced during your reading.

At the end of each chapter, think of a question or concern that the text raised for you. Take a deep breath or two. Look at the OH Cards. Do you see options and possibilities? A step you can take now that will make a difference?

Even after you've read the book from cover to cover, keep it with you. At any time, you can look at any of the chapters or card combinations to gain insights about the happenings in your life. You can even use cards from one chapter to explore questions raised in another. As you gain clarity, you may find yourself saying, "Oh!"

Illustrations of the OH Cards, created by Ely Raman, are used with the permission of the publisher. For more information, please contact Eos Interactive Cards by e-mail at info@OH-Cards.com or visit their website at www.OH-Cards.com

1
Spirituality
One of many paths

Spirituality doesn't come in a "one size fits all" package. My present spiritual beliefs were founded over many years of readings, discussions, and workshops.

One book, *A Course in Miracles,* has had a profound impact on my life. The assertions of ACIM that it was but one of many spiritual paths encouraged me to delve further into its teachings.

The lesson that has been my chief guide over the years is ACIM's definition of a miracle as a shift in perception. That made sense to me. I know that when I've stubbornly clung to a particular way of looking at a situation, I've mentally told myself that only a miracle would make me change my mind. Here, I'd like to share with you some of the principles that have helped me to change over the years.

Have you ever felt that you've wronged someone, only to have them brush aside your actions?

Years ago, a friend tearfully apologized to me for a comment made in anger. I had entirely forgotten the incident. I was therefore at first bewildered, and then amused by her interpretation of the event. She explained that she would have been offended if someone had made the same comment to her. To me, nothing had happened.

At other times, someone's innocent comments have triggered a very strong reaction in me.

According to ACIM, our responses to perceived slights and attacks reflect our projections or interpretations. Our responses are more about us than they are about the person that we are attacking or that we feel is attacking us.

We can choose to see our hurts differently. Forgiveness is one of the major principles in ACIM. Forgiving self leads to releasing others; forgiving others leads to releasing self.

ACIM is not unique in believing that keeping grudges enslaves us and that releasing grievances frees us. Many spiritual paths and therapies espouse this view. And it has major implications for healing.

According to ACIM, all healing starts in the mind, which is also where all illnesses (physical and emotional) begin. That theme is not unusual. Most holistic healing practitioners concur. Authors such as Bernie Siegel, Louise Hay, and Deepak Chopra, to name a few, write about healing minds and thoughts so as to heal lives.

The principle is simple but not easy.

I remember congratulating myself because I had been able to see that a friend's hostile actions were about her and not about me. Others may have felt that she had betrayed me, but I had not seen it that way. Then, someone cut me off in traffic, and the anger that flared up was incredible! Back to the drawing board...

Forgiveness is an ongoing process. It never ends. ACIM teaches that forgiveness is humanity's only function. Life can be a battleground where we fight, attack others and ourselves, and are attacked in return. Or, life can be a classroom where we learn to forgive and to love others and ourselves. It's our choice.

If we choose life as a classroom, we will continually encounter situations and people who push our buttons and trigger ancient reactions. We get to practice looking at those encounters not as attacks, but as fear calling for love. Gerald Jampolsky wrote a book called *Love Is Letting Go of Fear*. The title says it all, but the practice is easier said than done.

As a therapist, I have spent more than twenty years assisting people to let go of fear masquerading as anger, depression, and loneliness (among other emotions). Along the way, I've similarly helped myself. One of the principles of ACIM is that what you do to or for others you are really doing to or for yourself. It states that the therapist "learns through teaching, and the more advanced he is the more he teaches and the more he learns." In other words, we teach what we need to learn; and, in so doing, we are healed.

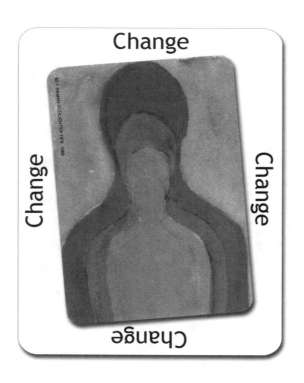

See page 14 in Introduction for suggestions on how the OH Cards (pronounced "oh" cards) at the end of each chapter may assist you in shifting your perception.

2
Spirituality
Taking the journey

It is easy to put spiritual work on hold when we're single and think that we need someone to complete us. That approach puts the cart before the horse.

Spiritual growth makes us whole in a way that allows us to make room for others in our lives. As I say elsewhere in this book, we're encouraged not to shop on an empty stomach because hunger causes us to buy everything in sight.

I have a wonderful friend who has the house, the cars, the trips—and relationships that don't seem to go anywhere. He's convinced that if he had a "special someone," life would have more meaning. As a result, he continues to gorge on external toys and desperate relationships that leave him empty. He sees the inner work that is part of the spiritual process as a waste of time. It takes him away from his external search for fulfillment.

No one can do our spiritual work for us. The spiritual journey is taken alone. But as we grow we are able to reach out to others from a position of inner strength. Miraculously, the strength attracts to our lives people and situations that enrich us, that challenge us, and that spur further growth. So, although we must do the work by ourselves, we're never alone. Along the way, we meet fellow journey-takers. These people enter our lives and stay for varying lengths of time. When the time is right, and we've learned what we can from one another, those people move on.

In his book, *A Path with Heart*, Jack Kornfield emphasizes the essential realization that spiritual process is not about possession of people or things. He goes on to say, "Spiritual joy and wisdom do not come through possession but rather through our capacity to open, to love more fully, and to move and be free in life."

That observation captures exactly why spiritual growth is a process and a journey. How many of us keep our hearts open, love unconditionally, and feel free in life all the time? We're all works in progress. At times, we may seem to pause, take detours, or backtrack. When those times come, we need to be gentle with ourselves. We need to find the inner voice that is not judgmental but that patiently encourages us to continue on the journey.

Being able to listen to the inner voice is essential. Sanaya Roman, author of *Spiritual Growth*, describes the process as a journey of self-discovery. You grow by "connecting with your Higher Self and to a Higher Power—the God/Goddess within and without, Christ, Allah, Buddha, the All-That-Is."

One way of contacting your higher self is to imagine that you have an inner wise teacher or guide. As you access and communicate with your inner power and begin to trust the messages that you receive, you increasingly experience the wisdom of the voice until it is who you are. You will have connected with your higher self when your dealings with self and others come from the heart.

Like most spiritual teachers, Sanaya emphasizes that enlightenment is not a place that you reach where growth stops and you are perfect. You always have higher and higher levels to reach throughout life. However, progression along the journey means that you acquire the tools and resources to deal with challenges met along the way.

The journey of opening one's heart can take many paths, but all lead to the same destination. I've been in conversations with friends who have tried to convince me that their particular path is *the* way. Do not be sidetracked by such talk. Find the path that touches your soul, keep an open mind, do your individual work. As much as possible, try to learn through joy. We can learn through joy or pain.

Many of my earlier lessons were learned through pain. As I have travelled my spiritual path, more and more of my lessons have been so easy as to have been a pleasure. I've also learned humility. Whenever I've taken my progress for granted, the rug has been pulled from under me quite swiftly. The resulting pain shocks me into the realization that arrogance has made me think I could travel alone, without acknowledging my ever-present higher power.

In one of her lectures, Marianne Williamson, author of *Return to Love,* described a relationship that "brought me to my knees." It was devastating. Yet she credits it with helping her go through what she calls *spiritual surrender*. That surrender occurs when you are forced to acknowledge that all your individual smarts and best efforts have brought you to a place so painful that you know that there must be a better way. Only at that point are we truly ready to take the next step in spiritual growth.

Marianne goes on to say that the spiritual path is simply the journey of living. "Everyone is on a spiritual path; most people just don't know it. The Holy Spirit is a force in our minds that knows us in our perfectly loving, natural state—which we've forgotten—but enters into the world of fear and illusion with us, and uses our experiences here to remind us who we are."

The reminder shows us the possibility of loving purpose in everything we think and do. Because love is our only function, it stands to reason that situations and people come into our lives to remind us of this.

Relationships certainly provide a major classroom for us to learn about love. Whether the relationships are with family members, spouse, partner, friends, or colleagues, they challenge us to keep our hearts open, to love unconditionally without expectations, and to keep a sense of freedom.

Marianne points out that all relationships are assignments. "They are part of a vast plan for our enlightenment, the Holy Spirit's blueprint by which each individual soul is led to greater awareness and expanded love. He brings together people who have the maximal opportunity for mutual growth. He appraises who can learn most from whom at any given time, and then assigns them to each other."

Marianne compares spiritual progress to detoxification: fear and pain have to be expressed to be released. Unhealed places must be forced to the surface to heal. When we are not in a relationship, we may feel that all the pain in life would go away if only we had someone. If we are being honest, we'll admit to ourselves that our relationships actually bring much of our existential pain to the surface.

I can remember speaking to an employee about work performance. Her response was a long story about how her mother corrected her when she was growing up so that, now, she didn't like being told what to do. A friend of mine once told me about a person that she took an instant dislike to. He reminded her of her father. After getting to know him, she realized that her perceptions had to do with herself and not with him. Relationships challenge us to use compassion, acceptance, and forgiveness of ourselves and others.

An old saying tells us that the world would be clean if each person swept the front of his or her doorstep. So it is with spiritual work. We don't have to save anyone—do spiritual work for them. If we accept responsibility for our own growth and life issues, our self-acceptance extends into acceptance of others.

Alone

Alone

Alone

Alone

3
Perception
The early shifts

Years ago, I attended a conference in South Carolina. There, I met a professor from one of the oldest universities on the continent. On my way back to Canada, we travelled on the same flight for part of the journey, and he entertained me with wonderful stories of his life.

The stories seemed straight from a novel. He told me of the time his fiancée's parents met his parents. A few months later, his father announced he was getting a divorce to marry the fiancée's mother. My new acquaintance related the events around the two weddings, his own and his father's, with humor. I plied him with questions, and he willingly opened up to talk about having five children and a PhD by the age of 32. His wife had just started her PhD at the time.

I learned that his children were now grown. They were professionally and financially successful. He laughed along with me as he described events that I would have found challenging, but that seemed to leave him undaunted. There was no mistaking the happiness in his eyes as he talked about his wife and children. I commented that he seemed to have had a happy life, and he affirmed that he had indeed been fortunate.

When I told him that I had always wanted to meet someone who was living the perfect life, and that he was that person, he grew quiet. He smiled and replied that he had never said his life had been perfect.

He told me that he hadn't mentioned that his mother had never gotten over the divorce. He added that he also hadn't told me about the time his house burned down and there had been no insurance to replace it. Nor about the time his daughter (now a lawyer) had been in a car crash and then in a coma for months. The doctors had given up hope that she would survive. She had survived, but she walked with a cane.

As this man related the other things that had happened to him, my envy of his perfect life changed. I became amazed that someone could have gone through such experiences and still describe life as being fortunate. I shared this feeling with him. He shrugged and said that the negatives were also part of life. He just didn't dwell on them.

That encounter reminded me of my earliest memories of the impact of changing one's perception. I was about 14 years old. Life felt very painful. I generally wore an unhappy face, and rarely smiled. When good things happened, I seemed unable to see them.

One day, a family friend gave me a story that she had cut out of a newspaper. It told of a girl growing up in an unhappy home. One day someone from her church ran into her. The girl was radiant. When the person commented that things must have changed at home, the girl replied that things hadn't changed but she had. That story gave me the first glimmer that my happiness was up to me.

My next breakthrough came two years later. I visited Jamaica for the first time since leaving the island as a child. My grandfather took me to visit an elderly couple in his neighbourhood. They were sitting on their porch drinking coffee. I was struck by the poverty that surrounded them. They seemed to radiate inner happiness as they greeted me. The wife gave me a big smile. She commented that the morning was good and that her coffee was "sweet and nice." Her husband nodded in agreement: the coffee was indeed very good and would we like some?

I remember thinking that it would have taken more than coffee to make me feel good. Years later, I understood those thoughts. I had been focusing on what was lacking in their lives, but they were focused on what they had that made them content. And at that time, it was a cup of coffee.

Of course it would be years before I connected the dots and realized the significant lesson in those three experiences. But I know now that seeds were planted then. And those seeds all pointed to a way of looking at life that has been expressed in numerous spiritual writings and by numerous teachers including Epictetus, Shakespeare, Albert Ellis, and Kenneth Wapnick.

For me the essence of that approach to life is captured best in this quotation from another of my teachers, Viktor Frankl: "Everything can be taken away but one thing: the last of the human freedoms—to choose one's attitude in any given set of circumstances, to choose one's own way."

4
Here and now
Casting a shadow

I remember being six years old and playing outside. I was twirling, going faster and faster, singing at the top of my voice. Suddenly my grandmother called out to me, "Chicken merry, hawk is near!" I paused, not knowing intellectually what she meant but instinctively knowing all was not well. I kept on twirling, more cautiously now, my singing not quite as boisterous. And full understanding hit me when I tripped and fell.

Thus goes my earliest memory of a lesson many of us learn in childhood. That lesson has many variations, but essentially it teaches that too much happiness draws danger or pain and leads to the loss of happiness. Over the years I've seen this theme play a major part in many lives, including my own. We pull away from joy out of fear of the pain that comes when joy goes. Because nothing lasts forever, and those whom the gods love die young, we learn to fear the good in our lives.

I understood Rita Coolidge when she sang that she'd rather leave a relationship while still in love. That way she could avoid the pain of losing love. Unfortunately, that approach leads to the very pain that one is trying to avoid.

A friend of mine once explained why his relationships never lasted very long. He said he always left when he realized he had started to care for the other person. His memory of an old relationship that started with stars but ended in destruction made him vow never to go there again. Sadly, by shutting the door on happiness, he was in perpetual pain.

The irony is that in our haste to protect ourselves from the hurts and disappointments that we think may come, we prevent ourselves from living in and enjoying the present. American writer bell hooks explains, "We have a history in this nation of believing that to be celebratory is dangerous, that being optimistic is foolhardy, hence our difficulty in celebrating life, in teaching our children and ourselves to love life." I would go further and say that this phenomenon isn't just American but universal. My fascination with this theme has caused me to ask people from different countries if their cultures had warnings about being too happy. Every culture had warnings of the dire consequences of having things too good!

For bell hooks, her wake-up call to stop and smell the roses came when she was gravely ill. She laments that many of us come to love life only when faced with a life-threatening illness.

Kate would agree with her. Kate ran into me, literally, when I was visiting Rhode Island once. After that encounter, we naturally struck up a conversation. I discovered that she started running after she was diagnosed with cancer. She changed her whole life, establishing a new set of priorities. The few months she had been given to live had now stretched into almost four years.

But she confided that she was still learning to live in the moment. She shared a conversation she had had with her personal trainer. He listened to her worrying about the fact that her illness and treatments had taken their toll on her. When she questioned him about how long it would take her to get back the strength and body she once had, he replied that as long as she had one foot in the past and the other foot in the future, she was casting a shadow over her present.

We cast shadows in life in many ways. I've heard many people declare that they wouldn't want sudden wealth because people who suddenly come into money either lose it or are cursed with disasters. We go through life longing for love, joy, and abundance...while fearing that we may get them. And we never get around to celebrating life.

Much is written about the fear of failure. But I say that many of us are limited by our fear of success. That fear keeps us playing small and avoiding the full enjoyment of the good things that come our way. A friend of mine has had many successes in recent times and has minimized them, playing them down. When I teased him about playing small, he gently pointed out the areas where I had been doing the same thing. (The list is much too long for this chapter!) I guess a part of me is still afraid of the hawk! Learning continues...

Now is a good time to express gratitude about the many good people and things that have been and continue to be part of our lives. It's a celebration.

Fear

5
Letting go
Confessions of a pack rat

I freely admit that I am a pack rat. The ability to throw things away or to let go of stuff has always been a challenge for me. Who knows when you might need it?

I remember years ago noting that I no longer recognized many of the things in my freezer. I reasoned that if something was in there, then at some point it must have had value, and so I should hang on to it. Over time, the containers took up more and more space, and clearing them out seemed a daunting task. I would open the freezer, stare at the contents, and then quickly close the door! Inertia had set in. I prayed for help to get me started in clearing things out.

When I went away on holidays, my sister offered to water my plants. During my vacation, she called with the sad news that the motor on my fridge had broken. Everything in the freezer had had to be thrown out. When she told me the cost of repairing the motor, it occurred to me that the help I had received in clearing things out was very expensive!

That brings me to another lesson I've learned. If we need to take action, the universe will provide hints, signs, and then nudges. If we still don't get the message, we get a shove. We can learn either through joy or through pain, but learn we will. The choice is ours.

My basement contained a lifetime of memories. It was a monument to what being a pack rat meant. From time to time I would try to clear it out, but I would get caught up in reading the books and magazines that I was glad I had saved, or in trying on the clothes that might one day fit me again or come back into style. After all, wasn't my daughter wearing my '70s clothes?

So nothing got thrown out, and, little by little, more was added. At times I would try to make some sense of my possessions. I would then be amazed at some of the treasures I discovered lost among all the clutter.

I gave away many bags of toys, books, and clothing. And still I didn't notice any change. I made plans to take my summer holidays and sort through the bags and boxes. I would give away or throw away the things I no longer needed. I would create a space where I could truly enjoy spending time. (I had also said this the summer before, but time has a way of disappearing...)

Matters were taken out of my hands when my basement flooded. The destruction was devastating. Mementos were sodden messes. As I tried to dry things that I could perhaps use, the clean-up crew warned me that mildew and the possibility of infection had made salvaging them impossible. Still, I was able to give many things away and to save some others.

As I watched a brand-new basement emerge, my wise son, sensing that a part of me was still grieving, pointed out that the flood had made it easier for us to clear things away. Now, we would actually want to spend time in the basement. True. But grieving is part of the "letting go" process. I was dealing with the overwhelming feelings of loss while feeling energized by the rebirth of our basement.

At last the basement was finished. I felt good about what we now had. Then, the basement flooded a second time.

Disbelief turned to resignation and later to acceptance. On the negative side, the few items I had managed to save from the first time around were now gone. On the positive side, not much had been left after the first time. I was learning a major lesson in non-attachment, an important step in letting go.

I am reminded of the lines in *A Course in Miracles* that say, "It seems as if things are being taken away, and it is rarely understood initially that their lack of value is merely being recognized." The book goes on to remind us that, as we go through the process of giving up the valueless, we learn that, where we anticipated grief, we find a happy lightheartedness instead.

If we resist the process, the universe steps in. We feel as if the rug has been pulled from under us, as if things are being taken away. We then have the opportunity to do the inner work involved in learning to recognize what we value.

What do we value? Clue: Look to the content—the essence—and not the form.

In the book *Tuesdays with Morrie* by Mitch Albom, Morrie says, "The most important thing in life is to learn how to give out love and to let it come in." As Morrie's body withers away, he reminds Mitch that "love is how you stay alive even after you are gone."

Love is the energy in the people and things in our lives. When the forms leave or change, the process of letting go becomes easier if we remember that only the love is real.

Hesitation

Hesitation

Hesitation

Hesitation

6

Here and now
Thanks, Little Richard

At the Blues Festival in Ottawa one year, I ran into an old friend. My simple question "How have you been?" generated a lengthy update on the pain this man had been experiencing over a woman he had rejected. He realized too late that he cared about her, and now he was in misery. All the women since didn't compare with her. He was definitely singing the blues and not having much fun.

He had also told me this sad tale the last time I had seen him. That had been months earlier, and not much had changed. I said a few encouraging words and moved on. I had a festival to enjoy.

Later, when Little Richard took the stage, I cheered. For me, that entertainer is a success story. I knew about the credit that he had not received for his contribution to music, the money that had never come his way, and the way he had been cheated as an artist. Now he was back on top, and this audience wanted to hear him. He was proof that you can hit bottom, get back up, and be a success.

Partway through the show, Little Richard reminded people that he had asked that no one tape or film the performance. He then went on to explain why. As he spoke, he became more and more angry and heated at the memories of the injustices he had suffered. It was as if he had gone back in time and could no longer see us. Instead, he saw the faces of those who had robbed him. In his intense pain and anger, he threatened to leave the stage.

Shouts from the audience to lighten up had no effect. He was on a roll. We were there to pay tribute to him as one who had been knocked down and managed to get up and thrive in an industry known for treachery. If he could do it, so could we. Instead, we were told that we were part of his abuse. It was time to leave.

On my way out, I ran into my friend of the unfortunate love life. He commented how sad it was that Little Richard was unable to move on and enjoy his life. Instead, the artist was stuck in the past, unable to enjoy present work and success because of old stuff. As my friend went on and on, I started laughing. I asked if his advice for Little Richard could also apply to himself. He too started laughing, perhaps for the first time that evening.

I suddenly felt a sense of gratitude to Little Richard. He had shown me a picture of what life would be like if I held on to grudges and grievances, and played over and over memories of the attacks and disappointments that happened in life. He had shown me what hell would look like.

I have had nights when the past has kept me awake, rummaging through my mind for all the things I should have said or done, or the things that others should not have said or done, or vice versa. Those were not good nights, but we all have them. Like Little Richard, when we get caught up in the maelstrom of misery and pain, we need a miracle to shift our perception. That night he was my miracle, a gentle reminder to me that there had to be another way of looking at things.

One of Gary Larson's Far Side cartoons has been able to help me shift my perception many times. It shows hell with all its flames, hot coals, and devils with pitchforks. In the foreground are two miserable, sweat-drenched individuals. In the center, a little guy is pushing a wheelbarrow of hot coals and whistling a tune, obviously unaffected by the intense heat and soul-breaking conditions. One devil points out my little guy and tells the other devil, "You know, we're just not reaching that guy."

I call him "my guy" because he's my role model. He's my reminder that I have a choice. I don't have to see myself in hell if I don't want to. Yes, people will cheat us, betray us, and leave us. And we will feel the pain of regretting personal actions. We need to look at those things and acknowledge what happened. But then, we must move beyond our battles and not dwell or wallow in the misery, because *that* is living hell.

Again, I'm reminded of Viktor Frankl's observation that the last human freedom is the freedom to choose one's attitude in any given set of circumstances. Thanks to Little Richard for reminding me that I choose the reality that I see, and that one possibility is to choose pain. Time to choose again.

Holding on

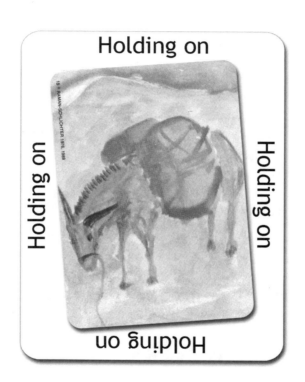

7
Forgiveness
The healing power of releasing grievances

As we move into the new century, we're at a powerful point to make choices and changes in our lives. Let's use honesty in our choices. If we decide to hold on to grievances and old hurts, we should acknowledge that we are the ones now causing our pain. No one is doing it to us.

A friend from way back carried much hurt and anger over the rejection she had experienced in high school. For whatever reason, one person stood out as the cause of all the relationships that hadn't worked out the way she had planned. He was the symbol of the cruelty that had affected her self-esteem over the years. Finally, she decided to confront him with the results of his callous treatment. When she went to look him up in the old neighborhood, his family told her that he had died eleven years earlier. He had truly "moved on," and she was still stuck in the past, replaying tapes of misery!

We find it hard to see that perhaps part of the poison and damage we're experiencing is not the result of the original wound, but of what we're doing with that wound. If we keep picking off the scab, telling stories of victimization and betrayal over and over to whoever will listen, healing will never happen. Instead, we end up with a festering sore that oozes toxin and poisons our very existence, making happiness elusive.

A client of mine once experienced much pain when her fiancé suddenly married her cousin. As time went on she stopped eating. Counselling wasn't reaching her. When I questioned her commitment to getting better, my client acknowledged that she didn't want to get better. She wanted her ex-fiancé to see how he had made her suffer. He was happy with his new family; she was willing to die to "punish" him. It was very difficult, but eventually, she was able to admit that, by failing to release the hurt she felt, she, and not he, was destroying herself.

The story of Bob illustrates that point very well. I encountered Bob at a conference given by Marianne Williamson in Toronto many years ago. Bob, a man in his sixties, stood up to share his very painful life with the audience. As we listened to his litany of woes, it became apparent that he had become an expert in telling his tale. Marianne's suggestions were greeted with more of his horror stories. Bob's interest wasn't in healing, but in exposing his wounds. Finally Marianne asked him to look around the audience and, as he did so, to tell himself "They too have suffered." It was as if a light bulb had been lit for him. He had been so wrapped up in his own misery that he had become insensitive to the feelings of others.

When we become like Bob, we believe that the only way we can be happy is to turn back time and to change the ending of the story. But changing the past is impossible, and so we replay the story over and over with others, hoping each time that we can come out ahead. Unfortunately, that approach only keeps the original pain alive. Moreover, we victimize others in our efforts to heal from a place where the hurt never happened.

If we have a choice between pointing the guilty finger or being happy, let's choose to be happy. It costs too much to tie up energy in making the other person wrong. It takes a tremendous amount of negative energy to keep the past alive in our present. In their book *Soul Dating to Soul Mating*, Basha Kaplan and Gail Prince say, "By holding on to past anger—reliving it, thinking about it, obsessing over it—we are never free from it. We give the past injustice power as we perpetuate it many times over. We need to ask, 'Does holding on to past wounds hurt the offender or does it continue to punish me?'"

If our choice is for happiness, we'll find that it is not on a straightforward path. Flashbacks, phantom pains, and backsliding will happen. But being committed to personal growth means that we'll be open to the many forms of help and support that come our way. The forms may be books, workshops, a therapist, a stranger on a train...or countless other means. All we need is a little willingness to continue on the path.

Habit

Habit

Habit

Habit

I remember hearing the results of a study on happiness being announced at the end of the news on a local radio station. The newscaster said that the study's findings showed that happiness was in the genes. The study had researched lotto winners and found that those who were unhappy before winning remained unhappy. Being able to buy it all hadn't made these people happy; therefore, they *had* to have been born miserable, sad little people.

But there is another way of looking at the findings. Becoming financially wealthy couldn't make the lotto winners happy because happiness is not about money. We need to take a different view of wealth and happiness.

A successful big-screen actress once told an interviewer that she was trying to figure out a way to make $100 million so that she could finally feel secure. Because of her "lack of wealth," she had taken roles in films she might not have taken had she felt financially secure.

Poverty, like wealth, is of the mind—a matter of perception. If we think we're poor, we are. A friend whose retirement income could support two families said that she'd love to win the lotto so that she could help others.

In shock, I asked what was stopping her from doing that now. After pondering my question, she replied that she supposed she could start. A year later she was still thinking about it.

Another friend wanted to follow her passion and start her own business. A cousin had tried the same field and failed, and so he warned her that she wouldn't make any money. Years went by, and my friend finally started her company. She told me that the passion and energy she feels doing her work makes her feel more alive than she has felt in years. Years ago I read a book with a powerful title: *Do What You Love, the Money Will Follow*. My friend didn't read the book, but she's living it.

I am reminded of something Debbi Fields, of Mrs. Fields' Cookies fame, said about the pleasure of doing what you love. She said her dad told her that if she loved her work she'd never have to work a day in her life. I need to be reminded of the pleasure of doing what I love because there are times when I focus on the fear. By alternating between fear of success (abundance would be too overwhelming for me to handle) and fear of failure (I'll become a bag lady if I "do what I love"), I managed to keep myself stuck with my wheels spinning. I discovered that I had an uncanny ability to scare myself silly with my imaginings.

Finally, I hired a coach. I told him that I wanted to finish my book and to increase my professional speaking engagements. He helped me to keep focused on my goals instead of my fears. That has made all the difference in my progress.

A statement by E.L. Doctorow has inspired me over the years. In commenting on the process of writing a book, he said, "It's like driving at night in a fog. You can only see as far as your headlights, but you can make the whole trip that way."

When we define wealth solely in terms of externals, we leave ourselves out of the process and a shrinking happens. We lose sight of what is really important, and we feel as if we can never have enough. There is an ever-present sense of something lacking—a sense of emptiness. It's like using a bucket with holes to haul water. The bucket will never stay filled.

You may remember the song "One Tin Soldier" by the Original Caste. It tells the story of the valley people who realized that the mountain people were happy and seemed to be having a good life. They were able to trace the success of the mountain people back to tons of riches that they kept buried under a stone. The valley people could imagine just how happy they too would be if they had all that wealth. So the valley people sent a message to the mountain people telling them to turn over their riches or die. The mountain people said they would be glad to share their treasure. That response so enraged the folks from the valley that they killed the mountain people. At last they could obtain the wealth and happiness that had been denied them. When they lifted the stone all they found was a message saying, "Peace on earth."

Wealth wears many faces, but we can know it is real when it begins within us. We manifest wealth when we stop using money or other external symbols as the barometer by which we measure our self-worth. We must work through the fear that says we're not enough and we'll never have enough. Then the abundance that may have seemed elusive becomes visible, and a belief in scarcity is no longer a viable choice. But the process is ongoing, and we're all on the journey. If the fear is too overwhelming for us to learn our lessons on abundance now, many other opportunities will present themselves.

Letting go

9
Emotional intelligence
On being intelligent

If you attended elementary or high school in the last hundred years, chances are that you've been touched by the tyranny of IQ scores. It means that, at some point, you were judged not smart enough and therefore headed for a life of mediocrity. Or else judged so smart that the world was your oyster. Either way, the potential seeds for damage were sown.

Many years ago I ran into a high-school classmate that I'll call Janet. She had excelled in school, and much to the annoyance of many in the class (me included), the teachers constantly held her up to us as a shining example. Her every statement was treated as a pearl of wisdom. When I ran into her three or four years after graduation, I was convinced that she had fast-tracked it through university and was doing her PhD.

Not so. She had had difficulty with her first year in university, had dropped out, and was then pregnant with her second child. What had changed her dream?

Years later, as a therapist in a university, I was working with many bright students who were ill-equipped and unprepared to handle the stress and uncertainty typical of the first year. They crashed and went into shock at the first sign of failure.

In our preoccupation with IQ, we have neglected to learn and to teach our kids about the essential skills of *emotional intelligence*. Those skills are not just about surviving, but thriving in life. Reuven Bar-on states that emotional intelligence "reflects one's ability to successfully deal with daily environment demands and, ultimately, influences one's overall psychological well-being." He designed the first scientifically developed and validated measure of emotional intelligence (EQ-i). Factors considered include self-regard, assertiveness, emotional self-awareness, flexibility, impulse control, and optimism, among others.

Of the fifteen factors that make up the EQ-i, one of my favorites is impulse control. Years ago, the marshmallow test demonstrated its importance. Four-year-olds were told that they could have one marshmallow right away or two if they waited until the experimenter returned to the room. Some couldn't wait; others could. By the time these same kids were in high school, the study showed that those who had been able to delay their gratification were among the best adjusted, most popular, adventurous, and confident teenagers. Those who couldn't wait were likely to be stubborn and easily frustrated. They also showed a tendency to avoid challenges and fall apart under stress.

Had I been given that test, I would have passed up the marshmallows altogether. I don't like them!

Impulse control carries over into other areas, and I can attest to the fact that EQ skills are changeable and can be learned. Over the years, I have learned, the hard way, the value of counting to ten, biting my tongue, and taking a deep breath, among other strategies. My kids are also learning.

Years ago my daughter had a teacher who was a work in progress when it came to EQ. One day she asked him a question to which he felt she should have known the answer. Because he had been having a rough day, he snapped that "any idiot" would know the answer. She shot back that that explained why he got it.

Had they been using bullets instead of words, both would have been seriously wounded. I'm sure neither left the exchange feeling good. The teacher ended up with a student who resented him for embarrassing her in class and who was reluctant to ask any more questions. The other students were also cautious in approaching the teacher because they didn't want the same thing to happen to them. My daughter had a teacher who felt that she was insubordinate. He never missed an opportunity to point out her mistakes in front of the class.

That lose–lose situation reminded me of a poem that I read in high school. It told of an inhabitant of a nearby planet. The being looked over to where the Earth once was and, seeing only a glowing mushroom cloud, murmured to himself that the ability to do that meant that intelligent life had been living there.

Emotional intelligence is crucial to our success in life. We can learn resilience, develop the strength to persevere, hold back, or change strategies to handle whatever comes our way. It doesn't matter whether the pressures come from a potential customer saying no, a public put-down from a stressed-out teacher, a failing grade on a project or exam, or a neighboring country showing off its strength by setting off a nuclear explosion. Whatever the form, our challenge is to shift our perception of the situation so we can look at the barrier or problem differently. We can then come up with solutions that show us the better way.

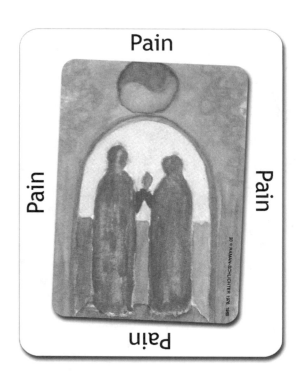

Pain

10
Strength
Of mice and men

Recently, I drove a friend home and waited to leave until he got through his door. As he reached the door, I noticed that he was shaking— with laughter! The next day he told me that I had seemed to be waiting for him to enter his home. When I admitted that that was indeed what I had been doing, he again broke out in laughter. He wondered what I could have done to help him if he had been attacked.

I could understand his skepticism: he was tall, worked out regularly, and was a police officer. I told him I didn't know what my help would have looked like. But I shared with him the story of a time when a friend dropped me at home and then drove off. That was when I discovered I didn't have my key. I had to seek refuge in a neighbor's house. I also added that, if he'd been attacked, I would certainly have been able to alert someone who could have helped.

My favorite Aesop's fable is the one about the lion who was about to snack on a mouse. But the lion decided to let the mouse go when the mouse argued that he could help the lion one day. That argument provided the lion with a bellyful of laughter. As he pointed out to the mouse, the fact that he was big and powerful meant that it was highly unlikely that that day would come. Still, he was now in a good mood, and he could afford to be generous. Later, when the lion was captured by a hunter's net, the mouse gnawed through the thick ropes and freed the lion.

Long ago, I learned that help comes in many guises. And that lesson has repeated itself many times in different forms over the years.

When I was in elementary school, Sarah was in my sixth-grade science class. She shrank from mixing with others and never put up her hand to answer questions. When a test was returned to me with a mark that made me want to cry, I asked the teacher to explain where I had gone wrong. He shrugged and told me to figure it out myself.

I can still hear Sarah's quiet voice offering to help me. How could she possibly help? She tripped going up and down stairs and, sometimes, even when standing still. As it happened, she had received a perfect mark on the test.

Decades later, we are still good friends and have helped each other through many of life's experiences. She may not remember how our friendship came to be, but I do.

Years ago, my spouse and I held a dinner party. One guest called up and chatted with me for several minutes. She then asked to speak to my husband, because she needed directions to get to our home. I obediently handed over the telephone. I took it back after my husband had explained to her that he had a poor sense of direction and that she'd have to get the instructions from me!

Life and literature are full of stories of people who were overlooked as expendable or insignificant only to turn out to be the person who provided essential assistance or held the missing piece of the puzzle.

Strength is not always announced with signposts and credentials. Daniel Goleman, in his book *Emotional Intelligence,* tells of a study that was done by Bell Laboratories. They wanted to see who the top performers were in the organization. Much to their surprise, the critical difference between those who were highly productive and those who were average had to do with cultivating good relationships with others. The telephone calls of the average performers were not returned, and their e-mail messages went unanswered. But the stars in the organization had built up a reliable network of colleagues before they needed them. When they eventually asked for assistance, help came right away.

Like love, help comes in many forms, shapes, and sizes. Treating others the way we would like to be treated and keeping an open mind are all the preparation we need to welcome it. Often it doesn't come from the direction in which we're looking; instead, it sneaks up from where we least expect it. But the help is there for us and reveals itself when we lose our preconceived ideas of what it should be. That is the miracle of expecting the unexpected!

Dream

Dream

Dream

Dream

11
Rejection
Overpowering rejection with curiosity

I had to laugh when I heard Marianne Williamson, author of *A Return to Love*, tell her audience, "If the train doesn't stop at your station, it's not your train!" Simple and obvious. Yet how many times have we railed against fate and events only to discover that not getting what we wanted was a blessing?

I can think of many times when I have pushed and struggled to have things go the way that I thought they should go. When I finally "won," I would discover that the train wasn't going in the direction that I wanted after all.

I can't say that it was the "wrong" train. The pain I experienced taught me about letting go, about trusting my inner voice, about patience, and other valuable lessons. But, my God, waiting for *my* train would have helped me learn the same lessons with *joy*.

The gratitude I feel toward the universe for not getting jobs I thought I wanted can never be sufficiently expressed. Only in looking back am I able to acknowledge that I would have died emotionally in those jobs;

they didn't fit the person that I was then, nor the one I would later become. But, at the time, I didn't know that.

That is where staying curious comes in. We have to trust that we don't always have the full picture. We often don't know what is in our best interest. And it takes patience to wait for new forms to emerge when we don't want to let go of the old dream that has just died.

Many people have discovered their spiritual path or life's work through relationships. Not because they have called on God in moments of great passion, but because the pain that they experienced when things went awry brought them to their knees in prayer for release.

Marianne Williamson credits the agony that she went through when various relationships ended with eventually leading her to *A Course in Miracles*. And that encounter made all the difference in her life, and a difference in the lives of many others, as she shares her spiritual growth through tapes, lectures, and books.

I once had a client who was heartbroken because a man who was physically and emotionally abusive had left her. She cried over her loss, saying that she'd never find someone like him again. I silently hoped that she was right. Years later, that woman was able to look back with compassion at her younger self—the one who had not known that her partner's departure was a gift she would eventually be grateful to have received.

When we try to hang on to what is no more, we put limitations on what can be. We are saying that, out of the universe of possibilities that awaits us, only a given person or situation will make us happy—even as we're experiencing misery.

In her article "Rejected? Lucky You" (*The Oprah Magazine*, May 2001), Suzanne Finnamore describes the devastation she felt when her boyfriend decided he still loved his ex-girlfriend and walked out. She cried every day for several months. She also wrote poetry. The poems were later published in *Ms.* magazine, and Suzanne's writing career was born. Her ex became a minister, and Suzanne freely admits that, given her personality, she would never have made a good minister's wife. However, she didn't know that at the time.

Suzanne goes on to talk about the four-month depression she went through after her agent rejected a manuscript with all the subtlety of a jackhammer. But after summoning the courage to approach other agents, she sold book and film rights within days.

Sometimes what feels like rejection, isn't. Staying curious long enough to find out can make all the difference.

The first article that I sold was to a major newspaper. Twice I submitted it to the editor, and twice he came back with criticisms and suggestions. I felt that he was trying to let me down easy, and so I put the article away. Weeks later when a friend asked me about it, I explained that the editor had not been interested. She laughed and said that his comments meant that he had done half the work for me. What a perception shift!

I resubmitted the article with the changes...and the editor bought it. I've been writing ever since.

Staying curious means acknowledging that we don't have all the necessary information about the past, present, and future. What looks like rejection might be that—and then again, it might not. Staying curious provides time for events to unfold and gifts to be revealed. It creates room in our lives for the richness that can be ours.

Retreat

12
Here and now
Hidden treasures

Years ago, I was going through one of those times when indulging in self-pity felt right. Here I was: widowed, raising my kids, and alone against the world. Nobody loved me.

As luck would have it, a particularly sappy song started playing on the radio just as I pulled into the garage. It was one of those "hurt so good" songs guaranteed to lower the spirit in the name of love. I decided to stay in the car and finish listening to it. I told the kids that I'd join them in the house later.

My son, who was eight years old at the time, asked why I wasn't coming in. I repeated that I wanted to finish listening to the song. He went into the house but, seconds later, opened the door to ask if I was now coming in. There is nothing like constant interruption to break a mood, and so I told him to close the door.

Seconds later, the door opened. He saw that I was still in the car. He turned on the light in the garage and quickly shut the door. He knew he was in trouble!

I burst into laughter as my "poor me" mood was totally destroyed.

Into the house I marched, and, with a stern look on my face, asked him why he had turned on the light. He confessed that he hadn't wanted me to sit in the dark. I laughed as I hugged him. Love was definitely in my life. It wasn't taking the form I was expecting, but the content was unmistakable.

Insistence on form can blind us to what is under our very noses.

Another amusing example happened to me when I was rushing out to give a workshop. A colleague had volunteered to print my handouts and leave them on my desk. As I examined the papers on my desk, my panic grew. The handouts were definitely not there!

My colleague then came into my office, took the papers off my desk and handed them to me. For years, I had printed these particular handouts on yellow paper. She had reproduced them on blue paper. What amazed me was the fact that I had actually picked up the papers and looked at them. I hadn't been able to see the content because the form was not what I expected.

A friend of mine recently ended a relationship with a woman who didn't fit his definition of beauty. His perception of her looks seemed to color everything else. As time went on, the flaws became more and more glaring. Only when he finally ended the relationship was he able to see the intangible gifts that she had offered him. And by then it was too late to go back.

There is a saying that the trick in life is not "having what you want," but "wanting what you have." Unfortunately, as Joni Mitchell sings in *Big Yellow Taxi,* we often don't know what we've got until it's gone. And by then, we've paved paradise to put up a parking lot.

I once had a client who was in danger of failing her academic year, so great was her pain over her parents' rejection. They had promised to help finance her education and had reneged on their word. This wasn't the first time: her life was littered with promises her parents had failed to keep. Fortunately, an aunt had stepped in and raised her with much care. But now her parents had failed her again, and her dreams of gaining their acceptance were once again dashed. She knew that they could have afforded to help, because they had recently treated themselves to some expensive toys.

I acknowledged that the cost of her education must be quite a burden for her to manage, but she assured me that it wasn't: her aunt was paying. The love in her life didn't come in the form of parents, but in the form of an aunt. No doubt about it, though—the content was definitely love. Her pain was causing her unwittingly to push it away.

This student definitely needed to grieve the fact that her parents were not capable of loving her in the way she wished. However, she also needed to move on, so that her loss wouldn't cripple her ability to be present in her life or destroy her ability to experience love. Her healing started when she was able to shift her focus from love lost to love present.

The many treasures in our lives can remain hidden from us if we have preconceived ideas about what or how they should be. Commitment to form causes us to miss content. Revelation comes when we keep an open mind.

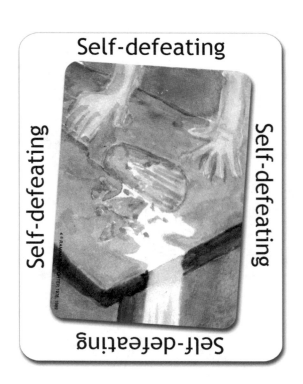

Self-defeating

Self-defeating

Self-defeating

Self-defeating

13
Scarcity
Two kilos from happiness

Recently, as I left a workshop, I complimented a participant on her outfit. She thanked me, but said that if she could only lose 20 pounds, she'd be perfect.

I had a quick flashback to a story a friend had told me three years earlier. She had been out shopping with her mother, who was going south for the winter. Her mother tried on one bathing suit after another, peering into the mirror and not quite liking what she saw. Something was wrong with each suit. Finally the mother sighed and commented that she would be so happy if she could lose two kilos. The patient sales rep shook her head and commented wryly, "Madam, we're all two kilos from happiness."

We see so much lack in ourselves that not only are we critical of ourselves but we are truly unable to extend love to others or receive it from them. In her book *All About Love*, bell hooks comments that self-acceptance is difficult: we've become used to an inner voice that is constantly judging us, and then others. She emphasizes that only when we begin to replace negative thinking with positive thinking will we realize that negative thinking is both unrealistic and absolutely disabling. She goes on to say that "when we are positive we not only accept and affirm ourselves, we are able to affirm and accept others."

bell tells of a time when she felt lousy about her over-40 body yet fantasized about finding a lover who would accept her as she was. The craziness of dreaming of someone to come along and offer the acceptance and affirmation she was withholding from herself did not escape her. It was then that she understood the maxim "You can never love anybody if you are unable to love yourself." However, she added another line: "Do not expect to receive the love from someone else you do not give yourself."

bell puts part of the responsibility for our state of lovelessness on our consumer culture with its heavy emphasis on advertising: "Keeping people in a constant state of lack, in perpetual desire, strengthens the marketplace economy. Lovelessness is a boon to consumerism." As long as we feel that something is lacking in ourselves, we go looking for it outside—a house, a car, a relationship, money, and so on. We hope that outward signs of success can cover up the inner self-loathing. Unfortunately that situation is a set-up for failure; we "seek and do not find." And so we keep seeking.

When my daughter Layla was about nine years old she begged for a Nintendo. She told of all the benefits and wonders that would befall our family as a result. And she promised to be good forever! Eventually she got a Super Nintendo. After a few weeks, when the benefits and promises didn't materialize, I reminded her of them. She commented in a voice heavy with disappointment that she had thought she would be the happiest girl in the world if she had the toy, but she now had the best one and nothing had changed.

I thanked her for reminding me that happiness isn't found in getting things. She was learning that lesson at an early age, and it has been repeated for her many times since. Teaching children to love and value themselves is not easy when we ourselves are learning the same lesson. How many of us truly believe that we have all we need? That there isn't something or someone out there that can complete us and make us happy?

That doesn't mean that we shouldn't strive to be the best we can, that we shouldn't pursue excellence. But we can do so with the voice of encouragement and care as opposed to the voice of criticism. In other words, the focus is not on what we do but on the thoughts and feelings underlying our actions.

We hear two voices that determine our actions. One voice rejects and devalues; the other accepts and affirms. When we bring to our awareness what we are hearing (from ourselves or others), we can then make a conscious choice to listen to the voice that expands our capacity to care for ourselves and others in a constructive way. Attachment to the outcome, whether it is losing two kilos, being in a relationship, or getting a new toy, is a good indication that we're coming from a place of lack and not of love.

What can move us from that place of lack? I can't say what works for you, but perhaps both of us can start with whatever affirms that we matter.

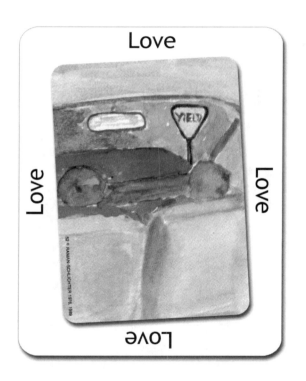

Love

Love

Love

Love

14
Fear
Doing it anyway

I remember reading the book title *Feel the Fear and Do It Anyway,* and thinking, "Easier said than done!" The title didn't mention that there is a crucial period between feeling the fear and taking action. Someone once called it "the dark night of the soul."

If you have ever experienced it (and who hasn't), you know what I'm talking about. I could have called this chapter "How I learned to ski from the top of the mountain." After years of enjoying the safety of skiing from the midpoint of my favorite mountain in Vermont, I decided to go to the top of the mountain. After all, my kids could do it, and I had started skiing before they did, right?

I remember the day vividly. I stood at the top of the mountain, and then I made a crucial error: I looked down. The view took on a nightmarish aspect as the mountain appeared steeper and steeper. I remember feeling the vibrations of my pounding heart as I started to shake. I knew I wouldn't make it down alive (by then the mountain had become a precipice).

I did all kinds of self-talk. I acknowledged that my mind was playing tricks on me. I reminded myself that the little kids I saw whizzing by were not scared. The more I tried to reason with myself, the more my panic grew. Finally I did the only thing I could do. I sat down and proceeded to slide and roll down the mountain! Once I reached mid-station—the familiar—I was able to ski the rest of the way down.

The next day I decided to retreat to a place of safety where there was no fear: mid-station. As I was getting on the ski lift, a woman came up and asked if she could share it with me. I inwardly groaned. I didn't want to go through the small talk of where I was from and what I did for a living.

But this woman wasn't interested in my life story. She wanted to talk about her skiing experience. This was her first week skiing, and she proudly told me she had skied from the top of the mountain two days earlier. I felt a mixture of disbelief and envy until she told me her story. Her husband had stumbled in getting off at mid-station and was unable to take their three-year-old son off the lift. She stayed on and listened to her son scream all the way to the top. The snowmobile could bring her son down, but it would have to make another trip for her. Her son's frightened cries convinced her to ski down behind the snowmobile. She never doubted that she could do it.

I was inspired. As I got ready to get off at mid-station, I asked her if she was going to the top. She looked at me in amazement and reminded me that she couldn't really ski.

That afternoon, I went to the top of the mountain armed with renewed knowledge of what I needed to do. I simply had to make my desire to succeed greater than my fear.

I'm reminded of why I learned to ski in the first place. As a therapist, I often see clients who are experiencing various stages of grief. One effective technique to help the healing process is to encourage them to start something that they've always wanted to do but have never made the time for or were too afraid to try. That exercise reconnects the person with self, and sends the message that he or she is alive. It also gives a sense of accomplishment.

When my husband died, I was frozen in pain. And so I took my own remedy. I remembered that my big fear was skiing. Six weeks later, I was on the slopes taking lessons. Skiing helped me to reconnect with life in a new way. It showed me that growth, learning, and recovery were possible. Years later, I was learning a similar lesson, but at a different level. My lessons were never about skiing; they were about facing fear.

We all encounter such lessons in many life situations. The time between the fear and taking action may last seconds or lifetimes. Life has given me an appreciation of the in-between space when the fear feels like it's raging out of control. That's when we need to remind ourselves that we've been here before and were able to move on. If we find that hard to remember, we can allow ourselves to be open to chance encounters, books, or situations that seem to appear at the right time to remind us. We can then do whatever "it" is, and move on to the next learning.

Disgrace

15
Emotional pain
Value in the valley

Years ago I attended a workshop where there was much discussion about enjoying the mountaintop, getting to the mountaintop, and staying on the mountaintop. Finally a woman got up and quietly told us that, with all the emphasis on the top of the mountain, we were forgetting the value of going through the valley. She talked about the lessons she had learned when she finally accepted that trying to rush through the valley was not in her best interest. The painful periods in her life had taught her patience and how to embrace herself as she moved through them. She could then appreciate the sweet sense of accomplishment as she moved up the mountain.

Another way of expressing her comments is that if you have fifteen tears to cry and you cry eleven, you still have four more tears to cry. So instead of trying to circumvent the valleys in our lives, we can pay attention to their teachings, learn their lessons, and then move on.

Certainly, staying in the valley too long can be dangerous. Wallowing in pain until it becomes part of our comfort zone can be easy and seductive.

I once had a client who was working through a very painful break-up. It was stirring up memories of other losses in her life. After a few sessions, she declared that the process was too painful—she had to stop the therapy. She added that she had looked at her friends and realized that they weren't all that happy. Perhaps she needed to accept that life was "like that." Getting comfortable in the valley can be as damaging as believing that one can live on the mountaintop permanently (avoiding life's challenges).

Unquestionably, the process of working through pain can be even more painful than the event that caused the pain in the first place. But, the process offers us an opportunity to do some housecleaning and healing that are all too easy to avoid when the going is good. Denial and avoidance are just some of the ways of going around the valleys we encounter. However, we can't deny or avoid for very long, because those strategies have ways of making life on the mountain less joyful. Eventually, we're plagued by physical symptoms and the signs of psychological starvation: depression, drama, and misery. That all-too-familiar feeling arises: "I have it all. Is that all there is?" And before we know it, we're back in the valley.

In her book, *By Way of Pain,* Sukie Colegrave talks about a woman who "feared who and what she might discover in the darkness, feared her own becoming, the responsibility for it and the demands it might make on her." Like the client I mentioned earlier, that woman wanted, in part, to cling to the old wounds—the neuroses and insecurities that were at least familiar.

Sukie compares clinging to the old to moving into a more spacious home from the old house of many years that is about to collapse. She urges us to get in touch with that unshakable knowledge that tells us it would be impossible to reconstruct and reinhabit the old house without feeling diminished and cramped.

That is why going through the grieving process is so crucial. I remember identifying with the pain I heard years ago in Richard Harris' rendition of Jimmy Webb's "McArthur Park." He sang about someone leaving the cake out in the rain. About how devastating it was, because it had taken him so long to bake it and he would "never have the recipe again." Curling up in the valley in a cocoon of pain may seem like our only option when dealing with loss. We want to cling to the old form, refusing to accept that it can no longer serve our purposes. But we need to allow ourselves the creativity and sense of accomplishment that comes with discovering *new* recipes.

Sukie Colegrave uses a beautiful metaphor that is worth sharing. "Flowing with our river's journey requires continual change and adjustment. For an attitude, thought, or desire which once nourished and enlivened us does not necessarily continue to do so. Often the opposite occurs. Instead of unfolding, it begins, at a certain moment, to cramp and crystallize. To keep living, therefore, we have to keep dying, shedding outworn desires, conceptions, and attitudes, even outworn relationships and situations, so as to make space for new ones to be born."

When we are in the valley, flowing with the river is what makes it possible for us to arrive at a point where we can start moving up the mountain. And, having been willing to embrace our pain—to go through death and rebirth—we discover a friend along the way: ourselves!

Naked

Naked

Naked

Naked

 recently came across a Sally Forth cartoon by Greg Howard that I had saved for years. It made me laugh just as hard as it did the first time that I had read it.

The cartoon showed Sally trying to cheer Ted up. He looked quite depressed and told her that he didn't want to be cheered up; he just wanted to wallow in his misery. Sally wondered why he would settle for wallowing in misery when he could "hunker in the depths of desolation, dejection and despair." Better yet, she suggested that he try to "sink inexorably in the sullen slough of despondency." As the tiniest hint of a smile started to spread across his face, Ted ordered Sally to cut out her suggestions. She was starting to make him smile! What a gentle reminder to me not to take myself too seriously—not to make misery a way of life.

I can relate to Ted. The familiarity of misery can be perversely comforting. I call it the "peed bed" syndrome.

When my son was little he would often call out to come into bed with us in the mornings. Some mornings, he wouldn't. When we asked him to join us, he would ask why we wanted him to. No matter what we said, he'd refuse.

I finally caught on to the fact that the latter mornings were those on which he had wet his bed. On those days, I couldn't get him to leave it. One morning, in exasperation, I asked him why he wanted to stay in a wet, smelly bed. He replied that he felt cold when he got up. Once he got up, he'd have a bath, and all would be well. But the period between getting up and the bath was very cold and uncomfortable.

A light went on for me. I realized that his behavior was a powerful metaphor for why it can be easier for us to stay in misery rather than face the transition period. Misery can be familiar and comfortable. Change, by its very nature, tends to be uncomfortable and unfamiliar. We therefore avoid the things that have the potential to make us smile.

A client remarked to me that, as she listened to the news one night, she couldn't help but notice that her life had become like the nightly news. Only the negative things that happened during the day got her excited. The good things were pushed aside as not being noteworthy. Mistakes were blown up into major headlines.

This fear of the good times also shows up in relationships.

By the time a certain client came to see me, she had been in one negative relationship after another. She had had enough. After much effort on her part, her attraction to men who did not value her lessened. In time, she met someone who could appreciate her. But something didn't seem quite right. She finally ended the relationship. Because things had seemed to have been going well, I asked what had happened. She said that he had been getting pushy. Concerned, I asked what he had done. She replied that he had brought her flowers! As she heard her words and saw the look on my face, she burst out laughing. Then she added that she'd give him another chance.

Terry Gorski, psychologist and author of *Getting Love Right,* tells of a client who always ended up with abusive men. When he probed further, he discovered that she loved to hang out in biker bars. Her relationships were heightened by the uncertainty of the situation. Terry was able to link the rush that the woman got from those relationships to her childhood with an alcoholic father whose moods were very unpredictable. The trauma and drama from childhood carried over into adulthood. She hadn't even realized it.

Much has been written and said about this dysfunctional approach to life. Fact is, changing is not easy. Forgiveness and a sense of humor have been the main tools that I have used to help myself. My spiritual approach to life emphasizes forgiveness. It allows me to be easy on myself when I spend too long in the "peed bed." I recognize the fear that immobilizes me. Forgiveness involves not only forgiving myself, but also releasing those that I've tied to myself in anger (which is also a form of personal releasing).

It all comes back to us. Whether we forgive ourselves or others, we benefit.

A sense of humor allows me to avoid taking myself too seriously. Once I got caught up in the drama cycle of feeling betrayed. I then became very upset with myself for not having seen it coming. A friend pointed out that I was beating up on myself. Then, I really started criticizing myself for beating up on myself. I should have known better; I'm a therapist! My friend burst out laughing as she commented that I was now beating up on myself for beating up on myself. The irony and insanity of it all did not escape me. I, too, burst out laughing. And the learning continues.

Laughter

Laughter

Laughter

Laughter

17

Emotional healing
On being a friend

W hen we're in emotional pain, there isn't a pill we can pop or a magic wand someone can wave to make our pain go away. A perception exists that, if only high self-esteem were instantly available, we could sit back and enjoy the good life. It's hard to accept that, while no one thing can make us feel good about ourselves, lots of little things can make a difference. However, the little things need continual maintenance.

A client once gave me one of the best explanations of the "feeling good" process. She had been bemoaning the fact that there wasn't that "special person" in her life. Her sense of self was at an all-time low. But she had a good friend whom she valued. When I asked her what she valued about that relationship, she told me that her friend listened to her, saw her mistakes and didn't judge her, made time for her, and didn't put her down. I suggested an additional reason, and she agreed: there was an equal exchange of energy. The sense was that they were giving to each other; no one was being drained. Because these were qualities she valued in the friendship, I asked her whether she was a friend to herself. She sadly admitted that she was not giving herself any of these gifts.

She was more than willing to cancel plans she had made with herself to make time for others. She often ignored her inner voice if it whispered that someone or something she wanted might not be right for her. She could beat up on herself better than any prizefighter, and her harsh judgments of herself were accompanied by critical self-talk. Her energy flowed out to others to win their affection, but she gave little to herself. No wonder she didn't like herself!

It is very hard to be a friend to others when we can't be a friend to ourselves. One friend disagreed with me on this point and noted that, although he was hard on himself, he was good to others and generous to a fault. What he didn't notice was the number of times he complained about how much he had done for others and how little he had received in return. He didn't notice how demanding he was of his friends. The one thing he couldn't give himself, or others, was love without strings attached.

A client of mine once expressed concern about her poor eating habits (she frequently skipped meals). When I suggested that she make a point of cooking dinner for herself, she looked at me in amazement and replied that cooking for one would be such a waste. The thought that she was waiting for someone to come along so that she could eat a decent meal had a profound effect on me. Her words encouraged me to make dinner dates with myself, to travel on my own, and to surprise myself with gifts when I least expect them.

Being our own friend means making sure that we have a support system in place. That system includes being present for ourselves and knowing when to reach out to others. I remember running into a friend whom I had last seen a few weeks before his wedding. Now, several months later, I offered congratulations and teased him that marriage had made him look great. I had never seen him in better shape. He then told me that his fiancée had cancelled the wedding three weeks before it was to have taken place. She had been in love with someone else.

Shocked, I stammered that he looked so good, happy. He replied that he had been fortunate to have had friends who listened to him as he talked about what had happened, over and over. And, he added, he had hired a personal trainer. His last comment made me murmur politely, "Oh yes?"

He laughed at my skepticism and said that, as he got into shape and developed muscles he didn't know he had, he realized that he was able to change, and he felt better about himself. So he kept it up and watched as flab became muscle. Then one day he realized he looked great, felt good, and the pain had subsided.

Self-care must be ongoing through good and challenging times alike. It's easy to ignore ourselves when all is well. However when we look to ourselves for support in times of need, we then find a stranger. Friends who turn to us only when the going gets rough aren't true friends. Self-care makes us a true friend. When times get rocky we will always have someone we can call on: ourselves!

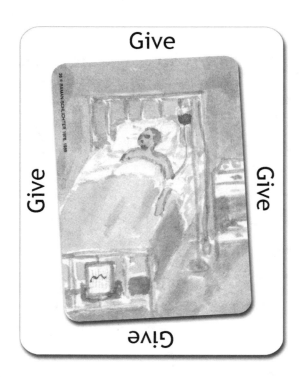

18
Relationships
Creating healthy relationships

Do you know what one of the major causes of loneliness is? It is the belief that somewhere out there waits a special person who will take away any sense of inadequacy, desperation, or emotional pain we might have.

Hooked on that belief, we go on a never-ending search for that person who will make us happy. When we find him or her, we run the risk of becoming doormats—looking after that person's every need while neglecting our own. Or we clutch and cling, draining the life out of the relationship.

We need to shift from looking for happiness where it isn't (externally) to finding it in the only place where it can be (in ourselves).

I've been doing workshops on healthy relationships for years. Participants often initially voice disappointment when I say that any relationship—whether with a spouse, a partner, a family member, a friend, a colleague—must start with self. Instead the people want to talk about how to find someone, how to fix the relationships, how to make the pain stop, how to keep someone from leaving. Because they are looking for a magic wand to wave away inner emptiness, they miss out on the miracle of truly connecting with others. Entering a relationship from a position of lack, with the idea of getting something from someone, is a recipe for disappointment and pain.

Airlines recognize the importance of self-care, of giving from a position of abundance instead of weakness. The crucial information that they give out at the beginning of any flight clearly tells you that if the cabin loses pressure, air masks will fall down automatically. If you're sitting with someone who needs your help, you must put your own mask on first. Then you can help the other person. If you fail to look after yourself first, you may pass out and be entirely unable to save the very person you're trying to help.

Also, keep in mind that desperation is just not attractive. Can you imagine saying, "I met the most wonderful, needy, screwed-up person. I'm in love!"

Guess who we attract when we're needy? Needy people! To have a healthy relationship, the first step is to make the shift from putting energy into looking for someone to love to becoming someone worthy of love.

Making personal emotional health a priority ensures that we allow into our lives people who value themselves and us. I've noticed that when my house is tidy, people come in and automatically take off their shoes. If belongings are scattered all over the place, people don't think twice about tracking in mud. How we care for ourselves gives others a clue about how we like to be treated.

Another strange thing takes place when we feel good about ourselves. We don't grab at the first person that comes along. We're not in a big hurry.

A friend once told me about an experience he had while traveling across the country. His vehicle had no air conditioning. By the time he reached a certain service stop, he was ready to drop from thirst and the heat. He bought a large carton of ice-cold milk and guzzled it down. He was almost finished it when he came up for air. Only then did he realize that the milk was sour.

We are advised not to shop on an empty stomach because we then buy everything in sight. That analogy also holds true for relationships (if you want a healthy one, that is). You know you're ready for a relationship when you're not hungry for one!

Expecting relationships to "fix" us, to make us feel better about ourselves, to fill whatever void we may perceive, is normal but not healthy. The search for emotional stability begins within.

Starting inside is not selfish. The ability to reach out to others from a position of strength instead of weakness is the kindest gift we can give. We can learn a great deal by observing life as it flows around us.

My godfather grows so many vegetables and fruits in the summer that he has to give most of his produce away. He gives me so much that I, in turn, must give much of it away.

True generosity is not about giving in order to get. Rather, it flows from abundance, from knowing that we have more than enough. There is no sense of lack, and we give freely. We don't need to clutch, grab, and manipulate others. When our relationship with self is healthy, we attract healthy people. And we will know the miracle of truly connecting with another.

Appearance

Appearance

Appearance

Appearance

19
Our legacy
The challenge of parenting

If ever I needed a miracle to help me shift my perception on a subject, it would be on parenting. As I've grown older, I've realized the importance of surrender: the idea that perfection doesn't exist and that all I can do is my best. But when it comes to parenting, I want to walk on water. Not only that, my kids *expect* me to walk on water. (And I must confess that I want *them* to walk on water too.)

I remember sharing my feelings with some friends. They were shocked to hear my thoughts, which echoed theirs. The sense of relief that we all felt was enormous. We were not alone. Finally, one woman humorously suggested we form a support group for misunderstood parents.

I remember a joke about a local politician who could never do anything right. Finally he hit upon a plan to get positive publicity: he would teach his dog to walk on water. When the dog perfected the technique, the politician held a press conference at his lakeside home. The politician threw a stick across the water, and the dog quickly ran across the lake to retrieve it. The reporters were amazed and wrote furiously about what they had just witnessed. Pleased, the politician offered to have the dog repeat the trick. Sure enough, the dog walked on water again. The next day, the newspaper headlines screamed the shocking news that the politician's dog could not swim.

Some days, I feel like that politician. How did it all start?

I saw an episode of *Sex and the City* in which Charlotte, one of the characters, expressed her desire to have a baby. After witnessing the dreadful behavior of some friends' children, she experienced a change of heart. Then we find out that Charlotte's husband has whispered to her those words that have allowed the species to continue: "Ours will be different."

I would add that some other words we tell ourselves accomplish the same trick: "I'll be different from my parents."

Years ago, I attended a workshop by Adele Faber, author of *Siblings Without Rivalry* and *Liberated Parents/Liberated Children*. One woman spoke for most of us when she talked about how hard it was being a parent. She wanted the best for her children, but she found herself saying and doing the very things that had really hurt her when she was growing up—damaging things that she had promised herself never to do or to say to her kids. She wanted her children to have a childhood different than the one she had had, and she now felt that she had failed as a parent.

Adele told her to honor herself for doing the best she could and to keep on trying. Adele explained that, many years earlier, when she had been raising her children, she had been part of a parent support group. The group members had the same concern about relating to their children. A wise mentor told the group not to be hard on themselves. He said that learning new ways of relating was like moving to a new country and learning a new language. As you become comfortable with the new language, you may make mistakes. Many times you slip into the old language. You may always speak with an accent. But for the children, the new language is their mother tongue.

To continue the metaphor of language, I remember childhood friends who had traces of the accents from their parents' old countries even though they themselves had been born in Canada. The parents' past could still be traced in those children. But while the accent spoke of where the family had been, it did not define the family's future in a new country.

In much the same way, my daughter is a mirror in which I can see the discrepancies between my teachings and my actions. I remember being shocked at a particular colorful expression that she would use—until I banged my hand and heard myself using the same expression.

We will never be perfect parents. However, if we can provide our children with love, they will be able to deal with our imperfections as parents, as well as their own imperfections and those of the world. As a result, we will have given them wealth without limits.

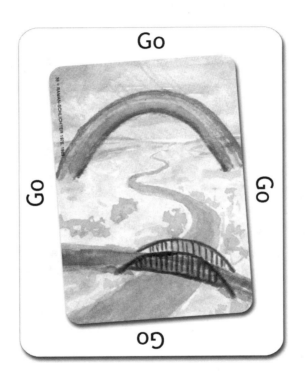

20
Security
The comfortable rut

A point comes in Shakespeare's play *Macbeth* when the witches are planning Macbeth's final destruction. They realize that if they are to accomplish their task, Macbeth must let down his guard and feel secure and confident. Hecate, queen of the witches, knows that success will be theirs once they give him a sense of security. She points out, "You all know security is mortals' chiefest enemy."

And we know what happens to Macbeth.

While we work toward security, a point comes when security starts to work against us. Complacency sets in, and initiative and personal growth disappear out the window.

In a workshop that I gave on risk-taking, one gentleman shared his dilemma with the other participants. He was now earning enough money that leaving his current situation would be very difficult. He felt trapped in a comfortable rut in which not liking his job was not enough incentive to leave. Someone else in the group mentioned "the security of the familiar."

Sticking with what is known may seem to offer security, but the damage it could potentially do to your sense of self and your ability to be all that you can be may leave you in a very insecure position.

That learning also applies to relationships. I remember an acquaintance explaining why she had left a relationship that seemed to offer happiness to return to a husband who was verbally and emotionally abusive. She said that she didn't know how the new relationship would work out, and so she preferred to stay with the devil she knew. Last I heard, her nightmare was continuing. However, it didn't seem to require her to make changes or to deal with uncertainty.

I suppose we can convince ourselves that there are benefits to be had in settling for less. We have a tendency to mistake stagnation for happiness.

An elderly couple came to speak to me at the end of a presentation I gave on the importance of being able to shift perception to see opportunities in life. The wife asked me if I could give a similar presentation at a later date, but with a focus on marriage. Her husband cut in to add that *they* didn't need such a session, because they had been married for sixty years. He felt that something had to have been working; they must have been doing something right to stay together for so long. The wife said nothing for a moment, but then repeated her request that I contact her if I intended giving a session on marriage. What was security for the husband might have been stifling for her.

Avoiding complacency doesn't mean that we should quit our jobs and end our relationships. Still, we can think back to a time in early childhood when falling downstairs didn't mean that we gave up learning how to walk. The pain didn't cause us to be paralyzed by fear.

Life's lessons are about getting up. If we focus on the spills and falls that are part of life's experience, we can miss the signposts that show us a better way to meet what we consider our challenges. Many past experiences in our lives and the lives of others can guide us.

I know that some people say, "Don't tamper with success," and "If it ain't broke, don't fix it." But there are others who say, "If it ain't broke, break it."

I suspect that the truth can be anywhere between those two recommendations. When things need to be left alone and when they need to be broken is a judgment call. A point comes when we need to trust our own inner guidance. That doesn't mean that we don't seek the counsel of those whose views we respect. However, by looking at situations from as many angles as we can, we can make decisions from a position of knowledge rather than a position of fear.

Courage is not about staying in or leaving a situation. It is about trusting that a force, higher than we, can help us to do our best every step of the way.

I remember a story that Marianne Williamson (author of *Return to Love*) told about a friend who seemed to have had everything in life. That friend then discovered that she had cancer. After various treatments, she appeared to be well on the road to recovery. However, she told Marianne that, while she had made many changes in her life since her illness, she would know that her recovery had gone too far when she failed to appreciate a sunset. That thought encompasses a call for balance and a challenge to discover what is authentic and meaningful in life. Those are the challenges of our personal journey.

Child

Child

Child

Child

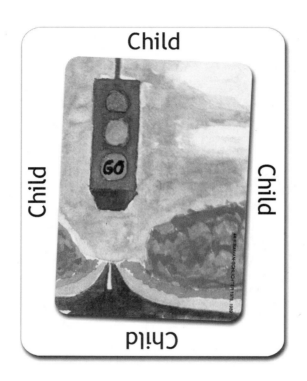

21
Here and now
No ordinary moments

A colleague recently came to work in a state of shock. The night before, she had rushed through dinner as she was working on an important project. She then decided to make some tea. She was good at doing several things at the same time, and so putting on the kettle while getting supplies ready for work was not a big deal.

But this time, she turned on the wrong burner and promptly left the room. When she returned to the kitchen, the Pyrex dish containing the leftovers was smoking. Without even thinking, she grabbed an oven mitt, picked up the dish, and headed for the kitchen sink. She never made it there.

The dish exploded like a bomb into thousands of pieces. Shards of glass pierced her clothing, leaving her with cuts to her neck, arms, and stomach. The gratitude she felt that her eyes had not been damaged was tempered by the shock that, in the rush to get things done, her distraction could have caused her serious injuries.

She had discovered that there are no ordinary moments. Even making a cup of tea involves living in the present.

Dan Millman made that same discovery about living in the present, and it resulted in a book called *No Ordinary Moments*.

One day Dan was practicing *Tai Chi* in the park. People stopped to watch him perform the graceful movements, but he was so focused on what he was doing that he barely noticed them. When he finished, he realized that they were impressed by his performance.

He noticed that one girl in the audience was particularly attractive. As Dan quickly pulled on his sweatpants, his thoughts were full of that girl and how to approach her. Unfortunately, he put both legs in one pant leg and fell flat on his butt when he started to walk. His pride turned to embarrassment, and the looks of admiration from the crowd turned to laughter.

From that ridiculous incident came the profound realization that changed Dan's life. "I realized that I had given my full attention to the movements of *Tai Chi,* but not to the 'ordinary' movements of putting on my pants. I *had treated one moment as special and the other as ordinary.*"

I had read Dan's book, but I had obviously forgotten the message. There I was, on the riding lawn mower, doing a task I had done many, many times: cutting the grass. As I pondered a situation that had come up in my life, I was dreading the action I knew I had to take the next day. Lost in unpleasant thoughts, I ran over a tree stump. That flipped the lawn mower, and me, into a clump of thorny bushes. I had painful scratches, and one thorn had broken off in my arm. It was so deeply embedded that the doctor at the clinic had to freeze and cut into the area to remove it.

As Dan's wise teacher told him, "Life is a series of moments. In each, you are either awake or you are asleep—fully alive or relatively dead."

I'm sure that we've all had the experience of reaching a destination and having no memory of what we passed along the way or how we got there. We have missed out on many journeys while our minds were occupied elsewhere. We want to quickly grow up, graduate, and get things over with. We don't realize that we are throwing away precious moments. We fail to treat the mundane with respect, and as a result, we say no to some beautiful sunsets and yes to some cuts and bruises. Dwelling on the past or getting caught up in what the future could or should be is not living in the *now*. The ongoing challenge is to shift our perception into the present.

Suppress

Suppress

Suppress

Suppress

25 © HAMAN-SCHLICHTER 1976, 1989

A friend of mine died a few years ago. She had been very ambitious and, if the truth be told, a workaholic. It was such a shock to her when the cancer was first diagnosed. However, the treatment seemed to be working.

During that time, she gained a clarity that had been absent for a long while. She had come face to face with her own mortality and realized that there was more to life than the corporate ladder. She told me that, when she returned to work, she was determined to make changes. Things would have to be different.

She spoke with enthusiasm about her new plans, made time for self and family, and acknowledged to all that titles, promotions, and the illusions of prestige were no longer essential to her life. Meanwhile, the cancer quietly spread throughout her body and ended her dreams of living life differently. People who knew her were shaken by her death and vowed to learn from it. We wouldn't wait for a catastrophe or crisis to shift our perceptions of what was important in our lives.

One friend, Jim, heeded the message. He started taking his kids to the market for ice cream. For the longest time, he was a model husband and father. And for a while, he refused to work his normal 12-hour days. We shared many conversations about our gratitude that we, at least, had been given another opportunity to make changes in our lives.

But time has a way of moving on. Yesterday's vows fade as we get caught up with the demands that we have accepted for ourselves. Jim's friends were jolted when he suffered a stroke. Again, we all nervously took stock of our lives.

So did Jim. During his slow and painful recovery, he made permanent decisions about his direction. He realized that some of those decisions could cost him his career. And he didn't care!

In his case, the company agreed to the changes and then promoted him. However, what was life-affirming for him was that he had established priorities and had been willing to stick with them no matter what the outcome.

Not all of life's reminders leave us bruised. I had a gentle nudge once when I went on a Caribbean cruise. I met many people who had the time to go on a cruise now that they had retired. Some said that this cruise was their first and that they were very excited. Were they going on excursions of the various islands? Well, no, that would be too taxing owing to their various ailments. I was moved by their stories of working hard and not taking much time for themselves until now. I was again reminded how easy it is to rush through life while putting living on hold.

Yes, we can plan for the future. But we can do that without becoming consumed by thoughts and worries that make today a worn-out blur. Stockpiling toys, gadgets, and "must haves" is no compensation.

I discovered a box of "essential stuff" in my basement years after I had thought I had a need for it. I had survived quite well without it in the end.

I've been inspired by stories of people who had to leave their homes or countries with only one bag. How quickly they realized what was important and what wasn't. If you had 15 minutes to leave your home for the last time, what would you take? If you had six months to live, what changes would you make in your life?

We certainly don't have to quit our jobs and move to the wilderness (although there are days when I'm tempted!). Nevertheless, *now* is a good time to pay serious attention to what your heart is saying. Most of the time we're too busy telling ourselves what we need, must have, or must accomplish. We apologetically put ourselves on the back burners of our lives. Today, we should listen to our dreams and hopes, and make a commitment to move them to the front.

Erotic

Erotic

Erotic

Erotic

23
Emotional healing
Life on the couch

The couch has long been a symbol of psychotherapy. I've grown up seeing pictures of clients or patients lying on a couch while a therapist scribbles furiously in the background. Or, if it's a cartoon, the client is talking while the therapist sleeps!

The therapist is supposed to have answers to the emotional pains we all experience at some point in our lives. As a therapist, I wrote a column in a local magazine that gave me a great opportunity to share the steps in the healing process. Interestingly enough, in the picture for the column, I was the one on the couch.

Sad truisms exist about the lack of self-care found in many professions. We all know about physicians who ignored their health and thus were unable to heal themselves, and about the shoemaker whose children had holes in their shoes. Focusing on others is an effective way to avoid dealing with our own issues. That is not to say that we should stop giving to others and instead devote our energies to gazing at our navels! It does mean that we need to give from a position of having—of abundance. And the only way to have is to be generous and caring in dealing with ourselves.

Personal generosity and caring have been common themes in my writings and in my workshops. Maybe if I repeat them often enough, I'll eventually learn!

A point once came when I found myself stretched to my limit and beyond. As requests came in to conduct workshops, I would immediately accept them. I found myself doing workshops during evenings and on weekends. Finally, I decided that I would no longer do workshops on weekends. One group wouldn't take no for an answer, and so eventually I agreed to do a workshop for them. When a friend invited me to dinner for the same date, I had to decline. She reminded me that I had said I wouldn't be doing workshops on weekends. Then, she made the mistake of asking me what the topic was. After a period of silence, I had to admit that the topic was "Setting Limits." And we both laughed. I told her I was giving the workshop because I needed to hear the message again.

When I help others to deal with fear (masquerading as anger, depression, loneliness, or jealousy, among other emotions), the lessons are there for me to learn too. According to *A Course in Miracles,* the therapist "learns through teaching, and the more advanced he is the more he teaches and the more he learns."

In other words, we teach what we need to learn, and in so doing, we are healed. I don't have an explanation for how it happens. I do know that often after I've racked my brains trying to solve a particular matter, I've relaxed with the thought that I'll meet someone who will help me find the answer. Inevitably, people walk through my door with similar concerns. As I help them go through the process of changing their perception of the problem, the answer appears, and both of us benefit.

I remember listening to the pain a client was experiencing as a result of an ongoing conflict with her mother. Each refused to see the other's side because each knew that she was right and the other wrong. As I worked with my client to honor her own feelings and then to look at the problem from different perspectives, she was able to open her heart to herself and to her mother.

And after one of those sessions, I went home and apologized to my daughter for my role in handling an impasse we had reached. I had been experiencing difficulties seeing life through the eyes of a teenager.

At the end of the sessions, my client expressed her gratitude for the help I had given her. I thanked her for her kind words and said that I too had benefited from our time together. She may have thought I was being humble, but I knew the truth. No one is healed alone.

We all have access to the truth that we need in any given situation. But accessing that truth is not always easy—which is why we need to hear the messages many times from different sources. Synchronicity provides the sources. People and things come into our lives at the right time with what we need. That doesn't mean that their problems (the form) are identical to ours. However, the solutions (the content) will be. Content will always be about removing barriers that block our awareness of the love we carry inside for ourselves and for others.

I'll be on the couch as long as learning is taking place. And we all know that as long as we're living, the lessons never end.

Confusion

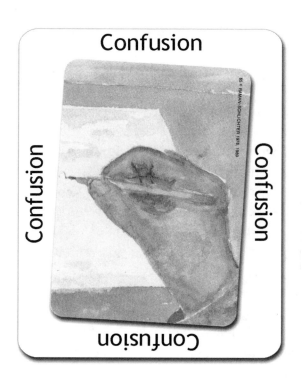

Confusion

Confusion

Confusion

Creating personal reality

Alan Cohen, author of *The Dragon Doesn't Live Here Anymore*, tells a story about a friend of his who wanted to clean her goldfish bowl. She filled the bathtub with water, poured the fishes in, and went off to do her chores. Hours later, she returned to see the fishes swimming around in the big bathtub—in a circle the size of their bowl.

A shift in perception requires us to do a little mental exercise: we have to look at a situation differently. First, we must be aware of the image that we currently have of the situation. Next, we must be willing to look at it another way.

How many times have we missed opportunities because we saw barriers that were actually flashbacks and no longer real? How many times have we been in pain over something said or done only to shrug it off with time? Time doesn't change the events: what happened is that our perception changed with time. And we can speed up time.

We can change our lives by learning from the universe. Physics teaches that we participate in the formation of reality. According to Heisenberg's uncertainty principle, quantum matter develops a relationship with the observer. It changes to meet his or her expectations. When scientists structured certain experiments to examine wave properties, they found waves. When they structured the same experiments to study particles, they observed particles.

We must therefore question what is real and what is reality. And we must be willing to accept responsibility for our roles as observers and participants in our personal reality.

Shifting our perceptions and expectations allows us to see what we want to see, and gives us a powerful tool for making changes in our lives. We may not have realized it, or perhaps we used it unintentionally—in a clumsy, haphazard way. According to Margaret Wheatley, author of *Leadership and the New Science,* "we do not, as some have suggested, *create* reality, but we are essential to it coming forth. We *evoke a potential* that is already present. Because things cannot exist as observable phenomena without us in the quantum world, the ideal of scientific objectivity disappears."

One winter a few years ago, when all the newspapers shrieked that there were no jobs to be had, a number of employers visited my university campus to recruit students. We were surprised at the low number of students who signed up for interviews. It turned out that many of the students "knew" about the job shortage. They figured the lineups would be long. Because they believed that their chances of finding jobs would be slim, they didn't bother to come out to meet the employers. By doing so they helped to create the reality of "no jobs."

We all have fish-bowl and missed-opportunity stories in our lives. Our challenge is to find all the barriers that we have erected to block our perception of possibilities...and to remove them.

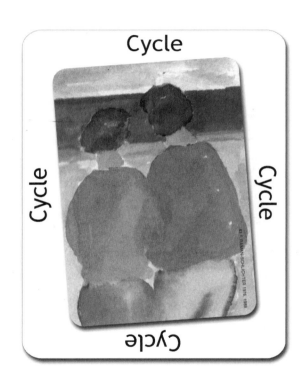

Cycle

Works mentioned in the text

Albom, Mitch. *Tuesdays with Morrie*. Rockland, MA: Wheeler, 1998.

Cohen, Alan. *The Dragon Doesn't Live Here Anymore: Loving Fully, Living Freely*. Somerset, NJ: Alan Cohen Publications and Workshops, 1981.

Colegrave Sukie. *By Way of Pain: A Passage into Self*. Rochester, VT: Park Street Press, 1988.

Faber, Adele and Elaine Mazlish. *Liberated Parents/Liberated Children*. New York: Grosset and Dunlap, 1974.

Faber, Adele and Elaine Mazlish. *Siblings Without Rivalry: How to Help Your Children Live Together So You Can Live Too*. New York: Norton, 1987.

Finnamore, Suzanne. "Rejected? Lucky You." *The Oprah Magazine*. May 2001.

Foundation for Inner Peace. *A Course in Miracles*. New York: Viking, 1996.

Gorski, Terrence T. *Getting Love Right: Learning the Choices of Healthy Intimacy*. New York: Simon and Schuster, 1993.

Gorski, Terrence T. *Addictive Relationships* (audio). Independence, MO: Herald House Publishing, 1986.

hooks, bell. *All About Love: New Visions*. New York: William Morrow, 2000.

Jampolsky, Gerald G. *Love Is Letting Go of Fear*. Toronto: Bantam Books, 1979.

Jeffers, Susan J. *Feel the Fear and Do It Anyway*. New York: Ballantine Books, 1988.

Kaplan, Basha, and Gail Prince. *Soul Dating to Soul Mating: On the Path Toward Spiritual Partnership*. New York: Berkley Publishing Group, 1999.

Kornfield, Jack. *A Path with Heart: A Guide Through the Perils and Promises of Spiritual Life*. New York: Bantam Books, 1993.

Millman, Dan. *No Ordinary Moments: A Peaceful Warrior's Guide to Daily Life*. Tiburon, CA: H.J. Kramer, 1992.

Roman, Sanaya. *Spiritual Growth: Being Your Higher Self*. Tiburon, CA: H.J. Kramer, 1989.

Sinetar, Marsha. *Do What You Love, the Money Will Follow: Discovering Your Right Livelihood*. New York: Dell, 1989.

Wheatley, Margaret. *Leadership and the New Science: Discovering Order in a Chaotic World*. San Francisco: Berrett-Koehler Publishers, 1999.

Williamson, Marianne. *A Return to Love: Reflections on the Principles of "A Course in Miracles."* New York: HarperPerennial, 1993.

Dawn Brown is an international speaker whose presentations are designed to inspire listeners and participants to reach higher levels of achievement in all areas of life. She is a member of the Canadian Association of Professional Speakers (CAPS) and the International Federation for Professional Speakers.

For more information on her seminars, keynote addresses and training sessions, you can communicate directly to:

Perception Shift
P.O. Box 64052, Holland Cross R.P.O.
Ottawa, Ontario K1Y 4V1

Telephone: (819) 770-3739
E-mail: dcosmob@hotmail.com